GETTING HEALTHY IN 7 SIMPLE STEPS

D1387347

Sarah Burt ND

Similia Publishing

Getting Healthy in 7 Simple Steps

By Sarah Burt ND

101 pages | 155g | 52 colour images | 4 b/w images
Original artwork (where indicated) by Sarah Burt
Photographs by Julie Bruton-Seal pages 56-61

First published in 2016 by Similia Publishing
Copyright © 2016 Sarah Burt
www.sarahburtnd.co.uk

ISBN-13: 978-1534976573
ISBN-10: 1534976574

Printed and bound in the USA

DEDICATION

This book is dedicated to the many patients whom I have treated over the last 16 years and to whom I have applied the tried and tested principles set forth in this work. It is the success stories recounted to me by those patients that inspired me to write the book you now hold in your hands.

DISCLAIMER

This book is intended to be reference work only, it is not intended to be reproduced, used to treat, diagnose or prescribe. The information contained herein should not be considered a substitute for professional guidance or consultations with a duly licensed health care professional.

ACKNOWLEDGEMENTS

The author would like to extend her appreciation to the following people, without whom this book could not have been written.

My sincere thanks go to:
Harry Burt, Andrew Mason, Howard Smith and *Julie Bruton-Seal*

With special thanks to:
Katrina Parker and *Aileen Kettle* for their unwavering support and faith in me.

CONTENTS

INTRODUCTION

Echinacea angustifolia

Is it really possible to become healthy in seven steps? Or is this book just another one of the many that try to sell you an ideal rather than easy, practical steps that will improve your health?

Are these steps easy to follow, or will they only work for people with eight hours free every day to dedicate to complex new ideas?

All the suggestions you'll find in this book are tried and tested. I promote them every day at my naturopathy practice and I've seen people benefit greatly from them.

Naturopathy is a health-integrated system that encourages people who are unwell to acknowledge the source of their ailments. Then, it offers ways to make changes in their diets and lifestyles that enhance the overall wellness of their bodies. Under these conditions, the body is able to heal itself in most cases.

I've been working as a naturopath and iridologist in the UK for sixteen years, running a busy and successful practice. I qualified in herbal medicine, homoeopathy, nutritional medicine, and iridology at the Australasian College for Natural Medicine in Sydney as Australia leads the world in complementary medical training.

During this time, I completed over 500 hours of clinical practice under the supervision of some of Sydney's leading tutors and practitioners. My course was just beginning to be accepted by universities and enjoyed degree status. However, the UK, still behind in its acceptance and integration of such studies, preferred to concentrate on orthodox medicine, which focuses on diseases rather than patients.

Hippocrates

Modern medicine is supposedly designed around the Hippocratic Oath, written by Hippocrates (460-370 BC). It includes these lines: '... with regard to healing the sick, I will devise and order for them the best diet according to my judgement and means; and that I will take care they will suffer no hurt or damage ... Nor shall any man's entreaty prevail upon me to administer poison to anyone.'

Even the modern day version, written in 1964 by Louis Lasagne, the then academic dean of the School of Medicine, Tufts University and recited by qualifying medical students upon becoming doctors, includes: '... I will prevent disease wherever I can, for prevention is preferable to cure.'

How many modern day general practitioners adhere to these words? How many doctors just prescribe a drug for a condition presented to them in their surgeries? How many people are prescribed antacids, statins, blood pressure tablets, antidepressants, steroids or non-steroidal anti-inflammatory drugs (NSAIDS) without any mention whatsoever of dietary adjustments first?

Surely, a person presenting with high cholesterol levels would benefit from an assessment of their diet? Surely, someone presenting with hypertension (high blood pressure) would benefit from dietary advice before any drug is administered? And so on.

Do you know anyone who takes prescription drugs regularly? Have they, to your knowledge, ever been given any dietary advice? I believe this should be the first line of treatment a person receives. It would reduce considerably the number of prescription drugs being manufactured and sold. It would also enable doctors to show that they're abiding by the Hippocratic Oath.

While I was studying Australia, the ideals in Hippocrates' original oath were very much being adhered to. By the early nineties, doctors and complementary thera-pists, seemingly at odds with each other's ideals, were working successfully together at health centres in Sydney, regularly referring patients to one another. As I write now in 2016, the UK still has much to learn from these partnerships. Being an old world country, it's often stuck in old ways and traditions. It finds it hard to welcome changes that can liberate us.

In my work as a naturopath over the last decade and a half, I've employed many new alternatives to orthodox medicines. It's been challenging. However, every patient I've treated is living proof that simple lifestyle changes can make a huge difference to health and wellbeing. And I'm extremely grateful to everyone I've treated for their openness and willingness to give naturopathy a chance.

In the following seven chapters, you'll learn about some of the techniques my patients have had the greatest success with. Combined with tailored herbal medicines, these have enabled me to treat conditions such as chronic fatigue (ME), weight issues, food intolerances and allergies, female reproductive complaints, fibro and polymyalgia, arthritis, irritable bowel syndrome (IBS), cystitis, allergic rhinitis, sinusitis, migraines, cluster headaches, stress, depression, anxiety, eating disorders and many more.

Each chapter covers a specific system. Together, they add up to a whole. By modifying that whole, we can make our lives happier and healthier.

I hope that, as well as learning much about naturopathy in this book, you'll also discover that making these seven changes to your life is far easier than you may think.

I'm convinced you'll enjoy the amazing – and almost immediate - changes you'll experience in your body and feel motivated to maintain your new good habits.

If you do, I believe your life will become simpler, less stressful, more joyful and fulfilling. After all, we're here for a short time really, so let's fulfil our potential.

We don't just owe it to ourselves to live a healthy life, but to future generations, too. If we can set a great example to our children, they too will grow up to enjoy healthy, happy lives, thus creating the blueprint for their children – and so on.

Issy and William

STEP. 1
ALKALISE YOUR DIET

No matter how different we all are, there's one single change that would benefit every one of us. To alkalise our diets. What does this mean, exactly? Should we avoid foods that are acidic in nature, such as oranges, grapefruit and lemons? No. The acid/alkaline balance in our bodies is still a relatively unknown subject. We don't fully understand what it means.

In my opinion, all disease comes from a root cause. More often than not, that root cause can be attributed to excess waste acid in tissue, known as metabolic acidosis. While we can test urine to see how many acid by-products it contains, we can't evaluate the state of our body tissues.

Diet contributes significantly to the build-up of acid in our organs, arteries, veins, skin, muscle and bone. By the time we feel the symptoms, our health is already compromised. When acid collects in the muscles and bones, aches and pains become more noticeable. A collection of acid in skin tissue results in conditions such as eczema, psoriasis, acne, poor wound healing or general poor skin health.

If acid targets the kidneys or the bladder, urine becomes more acidic, possibly causing a burning sensation as it exits the body. Reoccurring cystitis is directly related to excess acid in this area - and it can progress to more serious conditions affecting the kidneys.
Where acid targets the glands, these will swell uncomfortably in the neck, underarms, thighs and pubic area.

This, in turn, greatly reduces the flow of our lymphatic fluid, a viscous that removes toxic waste from our bodies. Our immune systems are then compromised, leaving us vulnerable to colds, coughs and ear, throat and sinus infections.

If acid decides to store in the blood vessels, arteries could harden and veins and capillaries may become brittle. This can predispose someone to heart problems and strokes.

Acid is corrosive. Wherever there's an excess of it, it'll try to eat away at muscle or body tissue. People with constant heartburn, acid reflux or irritable bowels are showing an accumulation of acid by-product. The whole of the gastrointestinal tract is made up of muscle that contracts and relaxes to push our food along. This process, known as peristalsis, is essential in maintaining proper digestion and absorption of all the food we eat. Without it, food would move erratically around our guts, resulting in alternating constipation and diarrhoea.

All seven to eight metres of our gastrointestinal tract is lined with cells that protect and soften, so food doesn't feel abrasive as it moves downwards. When these specialised (epithelial) cells are damaged by excess acidity, this protective lining becomes damaged. Acid then causes pain and discomfort, a feeling we know as heartburn or indigestion. Unless the underlying problem in corrected, rather than simply masked with over-the-counter antacid drugs, it will silently progress into a more serious condition.

The gut is lined with various forms of good bacteria. These eradicate bad bacteria that enter the body. Too much excess acid waste in the gut will overwhelm the good bacteria and allow bad bacteria to grow in their place. This is how a condition known as candidiasis can occur. Candida grows in all of our guts and isn't a problem under normal circumstances. However, it can overgrow, both externally, such as on the skin, and internally in the gastrointestinal and other internal tracts lined with yeast. Athlete's foot is an early sign of an imbalance which, left untreated, can progress rapidly to a systemic infection and enter all our internal organs. Topical antifungal creams, which are often prescribed for these conditions, merely treat the local area where the problem is showing, not the underlying cause.

Athlete's Foot

Serious erosion of the gut lining can cause a condition called leaky gut syndrome. An overly porous gut or bowel allows germs, toxins and undigested food particles to leak into the bloodstream. These particles then activate the immune system, causing inflammation in the body.

Problems caused by excess acid are initially minor, but become more serious over time. As it accumulates, acid becomes more aggressive and the symptoms worsen accordingly. However, by understanding the process, we can prevent build-ups.

It's vital, then, that we learn to read and react to the body's early warning signs sooner rather than later. Prolonged stress produces high levels of adrenaline in our body. The by-product of this turns to acid waste, which will attack our bodies in different ways.

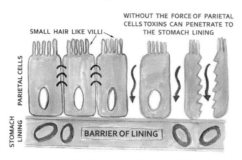

Leaky Gut Syndrome by Sarah Burt

Our bodies have an alkaline reserve to help neutralise excess acid. However, over-acidic diets and busy, stressful lifestyles mean that, for most of us, this reserve is severely depleted. The good news is that we can control the deficit. We can eat in a more alkaline fashion and, while we can't avoid stress, we can change the way we react to it. We need the systems that remove acid waste from our bodies to work well. Lack of water and fibre will cause a build-up of acid in our bladders, bowels and lymphatic systems.

The acid/alkaline scale

If a pH (potential hydrogen) reading of 7 is neutral, a reading of 7.5 upwards is considered slightly alkaline to extremely alkaline. Level 6.5 down to 0.5 is considered mildly acidic to extremely acidic.

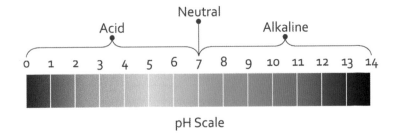

pH Scale

In his book, *Alkalise or Die*, Dr. Theodore A. Baroody sets out the specific pH levels of most of the foods that we eat. To simplify this, however, here's an overview.

Alkaline Fruits	
Apples	Limes
Apricots	Mangos
Avocados	Melons
Bananas [1]	Nectarines
Berries [2]	Oranges
Cherries	Papaya
Currants	Passion fruit
Dried dates	Peaches
Figs	Pears
Grapes	Pineapple
Grapefruit	Raisins
Kiwi	Raspberries
Lemons	Strawberries
1. acid forming if the skin is still green *2. except blueberries*	

Acid-forming fruits	
Blueberries	Plums
Cranberries	Prunes

Alkaline-forming vegetables	
Asparagus [1]	Lettuce (iceberg + leaves)
Artichokes [2]	Mushrooms [4]
Beets	Okra
Broccoli	Onions (including spring)
Brussel sprouts [3]	Parsley
Cabbage	Parsnips
Califlower	Peppers
Celery	Potatoes [3]
Chard	Pumpkin
Chicory	Peas
Corn	Raddish
Cucumber	Rhubarb
Eggplant	Seaweed [4]
Endive	Spinach
Ginger	Squash
Green beans	Sugar snap peas
Horseradish	Turnips
Kale	Watercress
Leeks	Tomatoes [5]

1. including tinned
2. Globe and Jerusalem
3. should be eaten with their skins on or they become acidic
4. an excellent source of alkalinity
5. depending on their sweetness, they range from 4.5 - 5.5. However people who suffer from gout, a well-known acid condition, all say tomatoes make the pain worse

Alkaline grains	
Millet	Quinoa

Note: due to the limited availability of alkaline grains, I usually permit small amounts of brown rice, spelt and corn products, which are acid-forming, in a person's diet. Barley, rye and oats are also only mildly acidic, so I allow limited amounts of these, too.

Acid-forming grains to avoid	
White rice	Buckwheat
Wheat	Couscous

Alkaline forming beans	
Lima	Soya [1]

1. and all other soya products such as tofu, milk, cheese and tempeh

Acid-forming beans	
Aduzki	Mung
Black	Navy
Broad	Pinto
Kidney	Red and white beans
Lentil	

Alkaline-forming nuts and seeds	
Almonds	Chia (sprouted)
Chestnuts (dry roasted)	Radish (sprouted)
Coconut (fresh)	Sesame
Alfalfa (sprouted)	

Acid-forming nuts and seeds	
Brazil	Peanuts
Cashews	Pistachio
Dried coconut	Walnuts
Linseeds	Pumpkin
Macadamia	Sunflower

Meat, fish and dairy products

There are no alkaline-forming meats. All meats and fish have pH values ranging from around 1.0 to 2.0. Other animal products such as butter, cheese, milk and eggs are also acid-forming.

If we drink milk, it's best to choose goat's milk. It's only mildly acidic (raw pH 6.7, homogenised 6.5) and contains high amounts of sodium, which aids digestion. Whey from both cow's and goat's milk is an outstanding source of minerals and nutrients, though cow's milk will cause more mucus residue. All plain yoghurt is only mildly acidic.

Neutral to alkaline oils	
Olive [1]	Corn
Almond	Safflower
Avocado	Sesame
Canola	Soy
Coconut	Sunflower
1. not for cooking, use coconut oil instead	

Alkaline-forming sugars
Brown rice syrup
Honey (alfalfa, clover and eucalyptus varieties)
Barley malt sweetener by Dr.. Bronner

Acid-forming sugars	
Artificial sweeteners	Molasses
Barley malt syrup	Maple syrup
Fructose	Milk sugar

Drinks

All wines, spirits, and beers are acid-forming, as are coffee, tea, carbonated drinks and artificially sweetened soft drinks. Herbal teas of all varieties are alkaline-forming.

Alkaline-forming condiments	
Agar agar	Sage
Cayenne	Tarragon
Garlic	Thyme
Basil	Vegatable salt
Chives	Soy sauce
Dill	Tamari sauce
Marjoram	Mayonnaise (homemade)
Oregano	Ketchup (homemade)
Rosemary	Spices [1]

1. includes: cinnamon, cloves, coriander, cumin, curry, fennel, ginger, paprika and bay leaves

Acid-forming condiments	
Gelatin	Mustard
Ketchup	Refined salt
Mayonnaise	White and red vinegar [1]
1. organic apple cider vinegar is alkaline-forming	

Recommended reading for great low acid recipes:
Honestly Healthy by Natasha Corrett and Vicki Edgson
Deliciously Ella by Ella Woodward
The Alkaline Cure by Dr. Stephan Domenig
The Acid-Alkaline Diet for Optimum Health by Christopher Vasey ND
The pH Balance Diet by Bharti Vyas and Suzanne Le Quesne
Alkaline Drinks by Marta Tuchowska
The Alkaline Satisfaction Cook Book by Marta Tuchowska

STEP. 2
HYDRATE YOUR BODY

Water ice crystal

The importance of water in our diet is grossly underesti-
mated. In our culture, tea, coffee, cordials, fizzy drinks
and fruit juices are generally the first liquids we reach for
when we're thirsty. Yet, starting each day with a pint of
spring water gets all the vital organs awake and working.
On the other hand, if we're not properly hydrated, we can
develop a whole range of common ailments – that we
seek medication for.

The medicines doctors prescribe for conditions related
to water deficiency are just palliatives (ie they merely
alleviate the symptoms). They're not designed to help
cure degenerative conditions caused by dehydration
such as:

- *Heartburn (dyspepsia)*
- *Hiatus hernia*
- *Angina*

- *Rheumatoid arthritis*
- *Migraines*
- *Depression*
- *High blood pressure*

All these conditions are linked to dehydration. Instead of simply drinking more water, people turn to their GPs for prescribed drugs such as antacids, blood pressure tablets, statins, beta-blockers, antidepressants and anti-inflammatories. None of these drugs will cure the condition – they'll just reduce the symptoms. The underlying condition of dehydration persists and more disease will develop in the body, which all the time is crying out for more water.

It's not easy to drink between 1.5 and 2 litres – that's around eight glasses - of water every day. Our taste buds are accustomed to sweet flavours and water is bland in comparison. However, squeezing a quarter of a lemon, lime or orange into a glass of water transforms it.

If you lose count of the number of glasses of water you're drinking, fill a 1.5 litre bottle with fresh (filtered if possible) water every morning and make sure it's empty at the end of the day.

The most common reason people give for not drinking more water is that they'd be forever emptying their bladders. This isn't the case. If we drink insufficient quantities of water, we never fully expand our bladders. And, like any other muscle that doesn't get regular exercise, it gradually weakens. So, by drinking more water and allowing the bladder to fill, we actually strengthen it so it can hold larger volumes of water for longer.

Thirst is one of the last signs of dehydration. To feel thirsty, we have to drink. We have a failing thirst sensation that causes chronic dehydration of all the cells in our body. We'll look at the early warning signs of dehydration shortly. But first, let's take a look at the damage it can cause (this is a great time to grab a glass of water!)

We have a thick, sticky mucus barrier lining in our stomach and it needs water to be an effective shield. Pain caused by dyspepsia is a sign that the lining is under

attack. Doctors routinely prescribe antacids such as Omeprazole, Lansoprazole and Ranitidine to alleviate heartburn, a symptom of dyspepsia, as these counter the excess acid the stomach is producing. But, if we hydrate sufficiently, we'll have no need for the millions of prescriptions given out for antacids - which contain between 150 and 600mg of aluminium in each tablet. Aluminium is said to be linked to Alzheimer's disease. Whether it is or not, aluminium is a poisonous heavy metal and we really don't want it in our bodies.

Only water provides natural protection against the acids we necessarily produce.

The cartilage surfaces of bones contain lots of water. This means dehydration can affect the way new cartilage cells develop and replace those that die and peel way. If a cartilage is well hydrated, it works smoothly, with no friction. If it's dehydrated and plump, abrasive damage occurs. Dehydration at the surface of a joint causes severe damage and can leave the bone exposed. This increases the risk of osteoporosis, a condition that makes bones become brittle and fragile.

Kidney damage is another effect of long-term dehydration. The kidneys are responsible for producing urine, which excretes salts and other waste material from our bodies. Urine output depends on water. Without it, urine becomes too concentrated and the kidneys can't cope.

Tea and coffee are dehydrating agents that have a diuretic effect on the kidneys. Excessive caffeine intake will also overstimulate the heart. In prolonged cases, this can exhaust the heart muscles.

Every function of our body depends on the efficient flow of water. All our hormones, chemical messengers and nutrients are guided around our body to the vital organs by water. If they can't reach their destinations, imbalances arise.

If there's a lack of fluid taking vital nutrients to our organs, there's also a lack of fluid to take unwanted products away from them. These by-products, (usually toxins and excess uric acid), are normally excreted by the kidneys and the liver. Without water to get them to the kidneys and liver, they'll eventually find their way to the bones, muscles, skin and glands. Here, they'll cause erosion due to their acidic nature.

By increasing the volume of water in our diet, we can prevent the build-up of acid in our body and avoid the destruction it leaves in its wake.

Cuenca Encantada (Spain) erosion of limestone

Early signs of dehydration

Pain arising from a cause other than injury or infection is most often due to a chronic water shortage in our body. Pain denotes the affect of chemical changes on the nerve endings monitoring the acid/alkaline balance in the affected area of the body. If there's no water around to wash excess acids away, the body tries to store them. The nerve endings sense the resulting acid imbalance and sends messages to the brain. So, the pain we experience is a safeguard against the build-up of excess acid by-products.

If we drink more water at this stage, the pain will subside. If we don't, it will persist until we take medication. It's vital, then, to treat this pain as the early warning sign and cry for water that it is.

Analgesic drugs, or painkillers, such as Anadin, Paracetamol, Ibruprofen, Nurofen, etc just silence the pain. They can also cause unwanted side effects such as increased gastrointestinal bleeding, which can be fatal. Other side effects include kidney and liver damage.

Overeating, a serious problem in many countries, is another sign that we could be dehydrated. This is because, in many cases, it's a misguided response to a thirst signal.

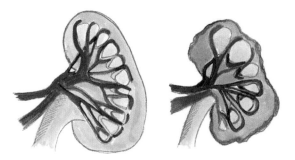

Healthy and diseased kidney tissue by Sarah Burt

Are you drinking enough water? If you answer yes to any of these questions you may need to drink more.

- *I get unexplained pain in any areas of my body?*

- *I get heartburn*

- *I get migraines, persistent headaches or a foggy head*

- *I sometimes experience constipation*

- *My urine is dark and strong in odour*

'Be sure to drink at least eight glasses of water each day.'

STEP. 3
LET YOUR LYMPH FLOW

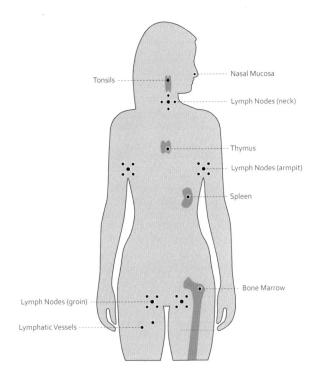

The lymphatic system is very much overlooked. This could be because few people really know exactly what it does. Efficient lymphatic circulation is vital to both prevention of illness and general healing.

The lymph system is made up of glands, lymph nodes, the spleen, the thymus gland and tonsils. It supports weight control, the immune system, the cleansing of blood and the detoxification process of waste from our bodies. It bathes our body's cells and carries cellular sewage away from the tissues to the blood. Here, this sewage can be filtered by the body's two main filtering systems, the liver and the kidneys.

So what is this sewage? It's the by-products of our bodily processes, over-the-counter drugs, airborne pollutants, food additives, pesticides and other toxins we inhale or ingest. The lymph system is also responsible for removing excess fat from our tissues. This means it has a big role to play in combating fat accumulation and cellulite development.

Normal tissue (right), cellulite tissue (left)

If excess fat is not removed, the body responds by storing more. Ann Louise Gentleman, author of The Fat Flush Plan, estimates that 80 per cent of women have sluggish lymphatic systems and that getting them flowing smoothly is the key to weight loss.

If you're suffering from injuries, excess weight, cellulite or pain disorders such as arthritis, bursitis or headaches, a sluggish lymphatic system may be a contributory factor.

Another main function of the lymph system is to pick up microbes, cancer cells and cell debris and take them to the lymph nodes where they can be destroyed. As the lymph nodes fill with bacteria or debris, antibodies will be produced within the nodes. This causes them to expand. We feel this as swollen glands. Any swollen

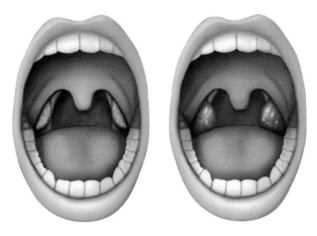

Healthy tonsils (left), inflammed tonsils (right)

tissue in organs such as the tonsils, adenoids or appendix will signal a blockage in the system. At this point, surgeons are inclined to remove these organs. Again, this symptomatic treatment will ultimately create more problems than it solves. Removing tonsils, for example, will further compound the blockage in the lymphatic system. This is thought to permanently affect lymphatic drainage from the head.

Glandular fever is a particular threat to the lymphatic system as it causes swelling of the lymph nodes. If the lymph system can't empty the lymph into the circulation, our bodies won't be able to dispose of dead bacteria. This could lead to swollen lymph tissue. Fluid can also accumulate in our system generally, causing oedema in the form of swollen ankles or puffy eyes.

If the lymphatic system is impaired in this way, the lymph fluid becomes thick and toxic, presenting the perfect breeding ground for infections. Then, when the toxic lymph returns to the general circulation, these infections are free to spread to any organ or part of the body. A toxic sluggish lymphatic system is at the core of fluid retention and muscle soreness.

Tell-tale signs that your lymphatic system is sluggish:

- *Lumps and growths*
- *Allergies*
- *Sinusitis*
- *Tonsillitis*
- *Enlarged prostate*
- *Heart disease*
- *Hypertension*
- *Eczema and other skin conditions*
- *Slow wound healing*
- *Repetitive infections*
- *Excessive swelling*
- *Cancer*
- *Ear or balance problems*
- *Teeth grinding*
- *Numbness or tingling extremities*
- *Frequent nocturnal urination*

Improving lymphatic circulation helps the body cleanse itself of toxic deposits. So, how can we do this? Through our diet, exercise, our lifestyle and, where appropriate, herbal therapies.

Foods that help circulation

Here are the top six foods for a healthy lymphatic system:

- *Raw fruit, eaten on an empty stomach – the enzymes in fruit are powerful lymph cleansers*

- *Citrus fruits - these aid hydration and carry powerful anti-oxidants and enzymes which help cleanse and protect the lymph*

- *Cranberries - good emulsifiers of fat, they help break down excess fat for the lymph vessels to carry away*

- *Leafy green vegetables such as kale, spinach, broccoli, mustard greens, and dandelion greens – they're rich in chlorophyll and have powerful cleansing properties for the blood, and therefore on the lymphatic system as well*

- *Nuts and seeds such as chia, coconuts, sunflower and pumpkin, etc for their essential fatty acid content*

- *Cooking oils such as olive oil and coconut oil provide healthy fats that fight inflammation and help remove soluble wastes*

- *Garlic, ginger and turmeric – they all improve circulation and support the cleansing of toxins from our bodies*

Herbal therapies for the lymph system

Herbs known to be beneficial to the lymph system include:

Echinacea augustifolia by Sarah Burt

Common name: Purple cone flower

Habitat: North American perennial grown on the India plains. Historically it was used to treat bites from poisonious snakes or insects. It was also favoured in the treatment of toothache, sore throats/mumps, measles and small pox

Action: anti-septic, anti-microbal, anti-viral and immune tonic

Echinacea augustifolia (echinacea) - best known for its immune enhancing benefits, particularly useful in reducing swollen lymph nodes.

Astragalas membranaceous by Sarah Burt

Common name: Huang Qi

Habitat: Native to Northern China, roots of 4-7 year old specimens are collected and dried during the spring. Huang Qi can restore T-cells to relativily normal ranges in patients undergoing chemotherapy, it also protects the liver from chemical damage during such treatments

Action: immune stimulant, cardio-tonic, adrenal and blood tonic

Astragalus membranaceous (Huang Qi), a herb the Chinese have been using for thousands of years to boost the body's life-force – it's a superb lymphatic system cleanser.

Galium aparine by Sarah Burt

Common name: Clivers

Habitat: Grows in the hedgerows and fields of Europe, North Africa and Asia. This 'climber' is well know by children for its stickiness, being covered in a multitude of tiny hooked hairs. Historically the whole plant has been used to heal and cleanase wounds, usually in the form of a poultice

Action: diuretic, anti-inflammatory and anti-bacterial

Galium aparine (clivers) – this cleanses the blood, the urinary tract and the lymphatic system. It also decreases congestion and inflammation in the tissues. Caution should be used with this herb if a person is diabetic.

Hydrastis canadensis by Sarah Burt

Common name: Golden seal

Habitat: a native American found growing in moist mountainous areas. This medicinal plant introduced to early settlers by Cherokee Indians who used it as an anti-bacterial wash for diseases of the skin, wounds and eye infections

Action: anti-septic, anti-microbal, anti-viral and immune tonic

Hydrastis canadensis (goldenseal) – for enhanced lymphatic clearing and anti-septic properties.

Baptisia tinctoria by Sarah Burt

Common name: Wild indigo root

Habitat: grows along the eastern side of the United States, frequently used by farmers to keep flies away from their horses. Historically, this plant has been used to treat aliments of the mouth, teeth and gums, the lymph nodes and throat

Action: anti-microbial, anti-catarrhal and lymphatic tonic

Baptisia tinctoria (Wild indigo root) – this helps eliminate microbes and cleanses the lymphatic system. It can improve lymph flow and reduce swelling in the lymph glands. It's also wonderful in the treatment of glandular fever and chronic fatigue syndrome.

Withania somnifera by Sarah Burt

Common name: Indian ginseng or winter cherry

Habitat: found in Australia, Africa and throughout Eastern Asia. Related to tomatoes, this plant produces small red berries about the size of a raisin. Historically, this plant has been used as a sedative, adaptogen and aphrodisiac, improving sexual vitality

Action: sedative, tonic, aphrodisiac, good rejuvenation properties

---

Withania somnifera (winter cherry) – is known to be an effective sedative and rejunvenative, acting mainly on the nervous and reproductive systems. Considered to be an excellent aphrodisiac, it is the herb of choice in Āyurveda for male fertility.

Note: herbal remedies should always be taken under the direct supervison of a medical herbalist / health care professional

---

Other ways to help clear the lymphatic system

Other good methods to insure you keep your lymph flowing include:

- *Drinking plenty of water to improve the viscosity of the lymph fluid - add freshly squeezed lemon juice so the cells in your body absorb it well*

- *Deep breathing - this will help move the lymph around the body. Try breathing in to the count of 4, holding for 2, breathing out to the count of 4 and holding again for the count of 2. Repeat three or four times every day for five minutes each time*

- *Exercise, especially bouncing on a trampoline - this really enhances the flow of the lymphatic system. Good stretching exercises such as yoga and Pilates are also good*

- *Massage, particularly specific lymph drainage massage - this will help get stagnant fluid back into the lymph system, break up toxins and enhance your mood*

- *Dry skin brushing with a natural bristled brush – work in short brisk strokes from the extremities towards the heart for three to four minutes. This works best just before a daily bath or shower and significantly improves the flow of lymph. It also helps soften skin*

One popular style of skin care brush

STEP. 4
REDUCTION AND MANAGEMENT OF STRESS

Of course, excess stress is bad for us. It's also an unavoidable part of modern life. So, in this chapter, rather than try to remove stress, we'll look at ways to reduce it through stress management techniques. First, though, here are a few facts about stress.

Stress is a normal part of life and can be experienced from our environment or in our bodies. It comes via our thoughts and emotional responses.

Stress is the body's reaction to any changes that require an adjustment. How detrimental it is to our health depends on the degree and the frequency of these changes.

The *fight or flight* reaction to danger/stress by Sarah Burt

Stress can be positive. It keeps us alert and ready to avoid danger. The fight or flight response (also known as the freeze and fawn response) exists for a good reason. It's a biological pathway that's triggered if there is danger ahead – and it makes us either run or fight.

In prehistoric times, this would be demonstrated by a cave man being confronted by a predator. He has a simple, yet urgent, choice - be eaten or escape / fight. This reaction, known as hormonal cascade, begins in the part of the brain that triggers the adrenal medulla, which releases the hormone, cortisol. This increases our blood pressure, giving us an enormous energy boost, which allows us to kill or be killed.

Once secreted, cortisol turns fatty acids into the energy the muscles need to prepare for this emergency response. Heart and lung function are affected, digestion slows right down and blood vessels constrict to list just a few of the physiological factors that occur at this stage. The immune system is also suppressed.

Stress becomes negative if we face continued challenges without any relaxation or relief in between. The continual raised blood pressure and tightening of our blood vessels will eventually affect our health.

Short and occasional bursts of adrenalin with long periods of no adrenalin in between are completely manageable for the body. What we're not designed for are continual daily secretions of cortisol into our systems. People who experience stress on the way to work, at work, doing the school run or in anticipation of challenging events have constantly frayed nerves and tensed muscles.

Adrenalin leaves a very acidic by-product in our systems that the body then has to dispose of. If this happens con-stantly throughout the day and the eliminatory organs can't cope with the volumes of the by-product, the body has to store it. Our survival instincts mean we keep this metabolic acid waste away from our vital organs and spread it around muscle, joints and bones instead.

To relieve stress, people often turn to substances such as alcohol, nicotine and other drugs, which they believe will calm them. Unfortunately, instead of helping, these substances only keep the body in a more stressed state.

At the time of writing, according to WebMD: 43% of all adults suffer adverse effects from stress and further 75-90% of all doctor's surgery visits are for stress related complaints such as:

- *Anxiety*
- *Depression*
- *Panic disorders*
- *High blood pressure*
- *Chest pains*
- *Irregular heart beat*
- *Insomnia*
- *Headaches and migraines*
- *Asthma*
- *Eczema*
- *Recurrent urinary tract infections*
- *Digestive problems such as irritable bowel, acid reflux, ulcers, weight loss and weight gain*

When we visit our GP's surgery with any of the above complaints, it's a rare doctor that suggests we first try counteractive measures to reduce the effects of stress on our body. The default response is to prescribe a drug that targets the symptoms.

Stress is a part of our busy lifestyles and we can't change that. But we can change the way we deal with stress.

We can choose not to resort to drugs that merely alleviate the symptoms of stress overload. We can implement lifestyle changes that include relaxation to counterbalance stress. And we can follow a diet low in stress-stimulating foods and high in foods that nourish and repair our muscles and nerves.

There isn't a quick cure for stress. Nor will any single method alone relieve stress for everyone. However, I'm sure that, among the techniques and ideas below, you'll find a combination that works for you.

Relaxed breathing

You can practise relaxed breathing in a quiet place where you won't be disturbed, in bed at night or first thing in the morning. It's also helpful when you're in a stressful situation such as driving in rush hour, taking an exam or preparing for a meeting or job interview, etc.

If you're sitting in a chair, avoid crossing your legs. If you're lying down, place your arms by your sides with your palms facing up.

Relaxation starts with the focus on breathing in and out slowly and in a regular rhythm. So:

- Fill the whole of your lungs with air, without forcing it. Imagine your lungs filling up from the bottom.
- Breathe in through your nose and out through your mouth.
- Breathe in slowly to the count of five, then breath out slowly to the count of five.
- Keep doing this for at least three to five minutes, two or three times a day or when stressed.

Deep muscle relaxation

This technique takes about twenty minutes. It stretches different muscles in turn then relaxes them to release tension from the body and relax the mind.

Find a warm, quiet place with no distractions. Get completely comfortable, either sitting or lying down. Close your eyes and focus on relaxed breathing as described above. You may need to practise these exercises more than once to feel the benefits. Next, work the muscles in these parts of the body:

- *Face* - push your eyebrows together, as if you're frowning, then release. Open your mouth as wide as you can then release. Repeat both of these exercises three times

- *Neck* - gently tilt your head forwards, pushing your chin down onto your chest, then tilt backwards without straining. Move gently to the left allowing your chin to lead the way, pause and come back to the centre before doing the same to the right side. Repeat three times

- *Shoulders* - pull both shoulders up towards your ears, hold for a couple of seconds then relax down again. Repeat five times

- *Chest* - breathe deeply into your lungs, hold, then breathe slowly out, allowing your belly to deflate as you exhale. Repeat three times

- *Arms* - stretch your arms in front and away from your body, hold, then stretch above your head. Hold this position, then drop your arms towards your feet. Stretch and hold this position. Repeat

- *Wrists* and hands - pull your hands towards you, stretching the fingers, then push away from yourself, holding. Rotate the hands at the point of the wrists, first in a clockwise direction, then in an anti-clockwise direction. Repeat for a minute

- *Legs* - push your toes away from your body, hold, then pull them towards your body and hold. Repeat ten times

Dambulla Golden Temple - Śrī Laṇka

Meditation

Meditation takes many forms, so I recommend doing some research to find the type best suited to you. You'll find all sorts of resources online, from apps - such as the popular *Headspace* - to YouTube videos and guides to meditation.

Bear in mind that, to be effective, meditation takes time. For this reason, you'll get the best results from a method you find simple and that encourages you to practise it often. Popular methods of meditation include:

 *Mindfulness* – created by Jon Kabet-Zinn in 1979, this technique is now offered in over 200 medical centres, hospitals and clinics around the globe. It uses breath awareness and body scan. Breath awareness involves focusing on your breathing as you inhale and exhale. Body scan means being aware of the body, starting at your toes and working your way up, relaxing the tension in each part.

Many busy people find mindfulness an excellent starting point, as it's very practical.

Note: An eight week mindfulness-based-stress reduction course is available a www.victoria.smisek.counselling.co.uk

Zen - also referred to as Zazen, which means sitting, zen derives from Buddhism which is a philosophy, yet often mistaken for a religion. It's accompanied by teachings (sutras) and doctrines learned through interaction with a teacher.

TM or Transcendental meditation was founded by an Indian yogi by the name of Maharishi Mahesh, this is based on the repetition of a series of Sanskrit words, or mantras, to help a person focus on meditation instead of concentrating on their breathing. A mantra is given to a person depending on factors such as when they were born and when the teacher trained. TM is a seated meditation.

 *Kundalini Yoga* - this meditation technique, founded by the spiritual teacher, Yogi Bhajan provides tools that support the mind and guide the body through the use of breathing, mantras, hand positions and focus. Kundalini yoga offers a range of techniques that can be tailored to tackle stress, addictions, low energy, low vitality and energy blocks.

Primordial sound meditation - this is a silent practice that, again, uses mantras. The mantra you're given is calculated using a mathematical formula dating back to the

Vedic period (cir. 1500-500 BC). Because the mantra relates to your specific time and place of birth, it's almost unique to you. By repeating your mantra, you're taken away from the intellectual side of the brain towards a deeper level of awareness. Like TM, it's done sitting down.

Whichever meditation technique you're drawn to, it's an opportunity to spend time in quiet thought. And the benefits are scientifically proven. One survey analysed 100 studies into the effects of meditation. They revealed that meditating - even for just 20 minutes a day for a few weeks – brings great benefits. They include:

- *Improved emotional well-being*
- *Increased mental strength and focus*
- *Improved memory and recall*
- *Better information processing*
- *Improved management of attention deficit hyperactivity disorder ADHD*
- *Improved immune system*
- *Increased energy levels*
- *Improved breathing and heart rates*
- *Fewer inflammatory disorders and asthma attacks*
- *Reduced depression*
- *Reduced anxiety*

Yoga

According to The British Wheel of Yoga, *'yoga is an ancient physical and mental practice, which has been used in the East for thousands of years.'* There are many schools of yoga, the best known being Hatha and Raja Yoga, (more commonly known as Ashtanga).

 Though it was probably around in the fifth and sixth centuries, Yoga only rose to prominence in the west the twentieth century. In Yoga, body, mind and breath are seen as unified in all humans and the system aims to cultivate our experience of that union. It seeks to bring about health and happiness using techniques such as postures, movement, breath awareness relaxation, concentration and meditation.

Walking

If breathing techniques, meditation or yoga are not your thing, you could do a lot worse than taking a daily 20-minute walk. If you concentrate on your breathing by taking deeper diaphragmatic breaths rather than shallow panting, the combination of the oxygen and the changing scenery will help to relax both your body and mind.

Foods and the nervous system

Foods beneficial to the nervous system include;

- *Anything rich in calcium, vitamin A and vitamin C, such as carrots, turnips and cherries*
- *Foods rich in magnesium, such as blackstrap molasses, millet and white beans*
- *Broccoli*
- *Swiss chard*
- *Red pepper*
- *Green pepper*
- *Kale*

- *Egg yolk*
- *Parsley*
- *Cantaloupe*
- *Tomato*
- *Sunflower seeds*
- *Red beans*
- *Lima beans*
- *Almonds*
- *Pecan nuts*
- *Hazelnuts*
- *Wild rice*
- *Lentils*
- *Oats*
- *Brown rice*

Consider also:

- *Spinach - it slows down the ageing process of the nervous system*

- *Whey - an excellent food with a naturally calming effect as it's rich in L-tryptophan. This is an amino acid which the body can't produce, yet is vital for the production of serotonin, our happy hormone*

- *Deep sea fish - these contains fatty acids, which line and protect the sheathing around nerves. Without this protection, nerves fray and become more sensitive*

Foods harmful to the nervous system include:

- *Bananas, figs, raisins and dates - these contain a lot*

of potassium, which can tire out adrenal glands

- *Refined flour, pasta, white rice, bread, and pastry - these cause a drop in blood sugar levels, potentially kicking the adrenals into unnecessary action*

- *Coffee, tea, chocolate and alcohol - these are stimulants so, as with rushing your meals, cause more stress in the body*

Supplements for a healthy nervous system

There are a number of dietary supplements available to promote a healthy nervous system. These include:

- *Vitamin C 1000mg with bioflavanoids*
- *Vitamin E 400iu*
- *Omega 3 (marine lipids) 1000mg*
- *Multi vitamin and mineral which contains good amounts of calcium, magnesium, selenium, zinc and all the B group vitamins*
- *Lecithin granules or capsules*

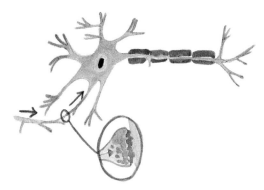

Healthy nervous system, neurons and synapses by Sarah Burt

Panax ginseng, also known as true ginseng

Panax ginseng

A herb I use in my practice sparingly, as it is quite strong in its actions as an adrenal tonic. I once used it on a friend who misread his dosage instructions and took double the amount. He later asked me if it was natural to feel like Superman from taking the herbal medicine.. his stamina was second to none and his wife was impressed to say the least. I think they were both disappointed when I corrected the amount he was taking!!

Cynara scolymus - globe artichoke

Cynara scolymus

Commonly known as globe artichoke, again the proper-ties of this wonderful plant I use much in practice as it is such a first rate tonic for any Gall bladder afflictions! My best friend suffers terribly with Gall Stone pain and just with this herb alone we have been able at first reduce and then alleviate all the awful attacks she was getting. As she is a busy mother of two gorgeous twin girls, she did not need the aggravation of these painful attacks so I have won a few favours from her by helping! As she is the best Reiki / Yoga practitioner I know, I've had no problem accepting her gratitude or in recommending her work, see: www.dorchesteryoga.co.uk/therapists/#annabelle-fox

Coconut drupe (fruit)

Coconut oil

So good for so many things, and now being touted as the oil to use... I find its actions most useful in reducing cholesterol in patients. It is mostly comprised of a type of fat called LAURIC ACID (50%) of its make up, which is a fat that is a good fat for our bodies and therefore offsets

57

the bad saturated fats in our bodies that clog our arteries. Being a good fat means it also supports the manufacture of healthy levels of hormones in our blood streams, also aids digestion of our food and boosts our immune systems as it is an anti-fungal, anti-viral and anti-bacterial agent.

Rhodiola rosea, also know as golden rose or golden root

Rhodiola rosea

This wonderful plant is again one of the top ones for adrenal and nervous system stress relief. It helps with stress, fatigue and depression. It helps with the latter as it enhances the transport of tryptophan and 5 hydroxytryptophan into the brain so that more SERATONIN our happy hormone, can be abundant. As serotonin is produced much better when there is adequate sunshine around, it is a particularly useful herbs to use in those horrible winter months when SEASONAL AFFECTIVE DISORDER is likely due to the lack of sunshine we get. So bear this in mind if you are someone like myself who gets S.A.D during the winter time!

Slippery elm powder

Wow! What a wonderful discovery this bark was going way back to the 19th century for the gastric system. We started to supply it at the Health Clinic where I work and for the first few weeks found it hard to keep up with the demand! Once people became aware of it, and heard of its uses to prevent acid reflux, Irritable bowels, constipation and bloating, people were coming from far and wide to purchase it, and were all reporting back with similar wonderful results. Most symptoms that people had been experiencing for years simply stopped! People reported back saying they did not have to take their medication for acid reflux any more.. so worthwhile trying out if any of those conditions mentioned affect you!!

It must be PURE organic slippery elm powder, some are mixed with wheat bran which will not have the same effect! You use one flat tsp, mixed with a little milk or milk alternative to mix it into a paste, then further add it to about a third of a pot of natural live yoghurt, then eat. Take this again in the evening, and watch as the condition goes!

For guaranteed good quality slippery elm please contact the practice managers at www.broadstoneclinic.co.uk where either Gemma or Amanda will send some over to you!

Schisandra chinensis, also known as five flavoured berry

Schisandra chinensis

This wonderful berry is known in Chinese Traditional Medicine, TCM, as 'the five flavoured berry' as it is bitter, sweet, sour salty and hot, and is such a powerful herb that it impacts nearly every organ and system... TCM hails it as a herb that can heal the three 'treasures' of the body.. and it has been called the Queen of Herbs before. I use it to restore liver, adrenal and nerve function mostly in my practice, although it also lowers inflammation, helps improve mental and sexual performance, and protects the skin. As it works on the liver, which TCM believes stores unresolved anger, I warn patients that when they start to take this herb they may experience anger over unresolved issues. So use it cautiously if this applies to you!

Eleutherococcus senticosus - Siberian ginseng (dried)

Siberian ginseng

Is another one of those priceless herbal remedies in any herbal dispensary. This is the female version of the afore mentioned adrenal tonic Panax ginseng. It is gentler in action, and works more over a long term, gently restoring the adrenal glands if a person has suffered with Chronic Fatigue for example. Safe to use on elderly and on children, this is the herb of choice for me when I treat children in Practice with Chronic Fatigue. It is wonderful with regulating blood sugar level and combats hight cholesterol too.

Allium sativum - fresh garlic

Allium sativum

Garlic is one of the most overlooked natural antibiotics. In practice I tell people who have bad sinuses or throat infections to cut three cloves garlic in half and swallow the bits, as you would pills. Often, this only has to be done once for an infection to clear. Garlic is also great for tummy bugs, its antibiotic and anti-microbial properties immediately killing any bugs, making it a useful winter remedy! Athough famed for its blood cleansing properties, garlic also has an ability to break down cholesterol in the arteries, making it one of our best (inexpenmsive) cardiovascular tonics.

STEP. 5
EXERCISE

There's something about exercising regularly that makes it hard to achieve. It could be the lack of time in our busy lives, medical conditions that limit us or the many excuses we can find not to take the idea of regular exercise seriously.

We may think a hectic lifestyle is exercise enough. However, being a busy mum running around after children, looking after a home or working in an office is not the same as getting 20 minutes of quality cardio-vascular exercise.

So what exactly is cardiovascular exercise?

Put simply, cardiovascular exercise is any exercise that raises your heart rate. Movement strengthens muscles - and the heart is just one big muscle. If we work it, we strengthen it like we do any other muscle in the body. A stronger heart means more capillaries (tiny blood vessels), delivering more oxygen to all the cells in our body. And this allows us to burn more fat during exercise.

We burn fat at the most optimum and healthy level when our rate reaches its resting rate plus 50 per cent. This is why simply being busy at the office or at home isn't good enough as a form of exercise.

We all have different target heart rates. You can work yours out using a specific calculator on websites such as www.healthstatus.com/calculators.

Modern exercise machines often show your heart rate while you're working out. However, if you're taking exercise away from such a machine, you'll need to learn how increases in your heart rate equate to how you're feeling.

In general, an elevation in heart rate coincides with moderate sweating while you're exercising. If you struggle to finish a sentence, the chances are you're overdoing it slightly.

Great ways to get cardiovascular exercise include:

- *Brisk walking*
- *Slow jogging*
- *Cycling*
- *Swimming*
- *Rowing*
- *Trampolining*
- *Skipping*

The American College of Sports Medicine recommends we take 30 minutes of moderate physical activity on most days. If this sounds like a lot, remember it's a mere half an hour in a 12–16 hour day and that exercise delivers all the benefits set out below.

Exercise burns fat

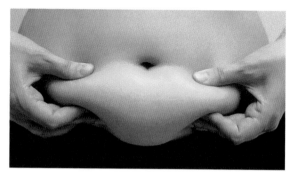

Ecxess belly fat

When we exercise, we burn calories. And the more intense the activity, the more calories we burn. Excess fat is stored around our vital organs. It wraps itself around the heart, liver, kidneys and pancreas and streaks itself through our muscles. This type of fat is called visceral fat and it's dangerously toxic. Far worse than just a lump of lard surrounding an organ, visceral fat is, according to Dr. David Haslam, clinical director of the National Obesity Forum, '... highly active and constantly pumping poisons into the bloodstream'. It causes inflammation in the colon, which can lead to cancer forming there. It causes the same inflammation in artery walls and is a major cause of heart disease and diabetes.

The good news is that simple diet and lifestyle changes can reduce visceral fat significantly - and quickly. Studies carried out at Hammersmith Hospital in London, for example, show that it will start to disappear as soon as a person reduces the fat in their diet and starts some form of physical activity.

Blood tests at the hospital showed metabolic changes in people's visceral fat within an hour of them starting exercise. This is because exercise targets this type of fat as soon as it starts and we begin digesting it almost immediately.
So, knowing that it really is this easy to tackle stored fat so quickly, surely the idea of doing regular exercise becomes more appealing?

Exercise improves your mood

Because physical exercise stimulates chemicals in the brain called endorphins, even a brisk 30-minute walk can make us feel happier and more relaxed. By exercising regularly and feeling better about your physique, your confidence and self-esteem will improve.

Exercise combats illness

Regular exercise can help prevent or manage a huge variety of health problems, most commonly:

- *Heart disease*
- *Strokes*
- *Type 2 diabetes*
- *Depression*
- *Arthritis*
- *Metabolic disorders such as conditions associated with thyroid underactivity*

Exercise boosts energy

Regular physical activity improves muscle strength and boosts your endurance levels. During exercise, oxygen and nutrients are delivered to body tissue. This both nourishes the tissue and takes rubbish away from it. This way, all the body's organs get cleansed and conditioned by oxygenated and nutrient-rich blood. Our body feels vital, fresh and alive and our energy levels rise as a result.

Exercise helps you sleep better

Without doubt, exercise will help improve the quality of the sleep you get. The kickback of immense amounts of oxygen circulating in our systems is a naturally relaxed state that encourages the body to need downtime every night. Muscles are more relaxed so stress and tension are less likely to keep us awake.

At the same time, our active mind - so often hard to switch off - is ready to rest. There's nothing more frustrating than being tired and weary, but unable to switch off mentally. Or falling asleep quickly only to wake up just a few hours later with your mind buzzing. The excess mental energy that robs you of sleep at night could be burnt off by simple exercise during the day.
So, bottom line, no excuses!

Whether you ride, walk, swim, go to the gym, skip, trampoline or exercise to home DVDs, be sure to get your 20–30 minutes of daily exercise.

NHS cardio workout

The NHS website offers a range of 10-minute cardiovascular workouts that you can download and get started on right now. Just type nhs cardio workout or something similar into your search engine to navigate to the relevant page. Then, all you need to do is find a way to slot half an hour of exercise into your daily routine - and make it as important as brushing your teeth.

No excuses. Just do it. It will change your life!

Exercise girl by Sarah Burt

STEP. 6
DETOXIFICATION REGIMES

Bio-hazard symbol

Hectic lifestyles, the modern diet and the chemicals and pollutants, etc we breathe in all exact a constant toll on our eliminatory systems. Our livers, kidneys, skin, lymphatic systems and colons are more overloaded than ever before.

However, by following a simple detoxification regime from time to time, we can give these vital organs and systems a chance to recuperate and regenerate. Detoxing can be highly beneficial, providing you follow a well-organised detox programme.

On the other hand, if it's not done properly, detoxing can leaving you feeling tired, bloated or unwell. It's therefore important, whichever method you choose, to ease yourself in slowly and adhere to the recommended preparation programme in the days before you start.

Typically, this will involve removing certain foods and drinks from your diet up to three days before the detox begins. These include coffee, alcohol, sugar, wheat, dairy, meat and tea. Additionally, avoid packaged, boxed, canned or fast food during the period leading up to the detox, too.

You'll also discover that, as well as cleansing your body's vital organs, detoxing offers a whole range of extra benefits that you'll really enjoy. Read on.

Detoxing boosts energy

When you detox, you'll replace caffeine, sugar and saturated fats in your diet with fresh fruit and vegetables, herbal teas and unsaturated fats. This will give you natural energy instead of the artificial type that gets used up quickly and leaves a slump in its wake.

Detoxing rids the body of excess waste products

Detoxing gives the body time to turn its attention to the waste toxins it has been storing. If left to their own devices, these toxins can leave areas in our bodies vulnerable to disease. By ridding ourselves of these stored toxins, we reduce this risk.

Detoxing helps with weight loss

We eat healthier food during a detox. This means we shed pounds in excess weight. Some of this weight will be retained water, but most of the loss is due to eating lower calorie foods than we would under our normal diet. It doesn't feel like we're dieting as we're not in any way restricting the amount of food we eat - just the number of unhealthy calories.

Detoxing strengthens the body

As our organs start functioning properly again, they begin to absorb nutrients more efficiently. This gives our immune systems a real boost. Plus, if we supplement the detox with herbal remedies to support the lymphatic system, we can improve our immune function even further. Even better still, taking light exercise as well will enable the lymphatic system to drain stored toxins faster.

Detoxing improves the skin

The skin is one of our biggest eliminatory systems. When we detox, it releases many toxins stored directly beneath its surface. For this reason, itchiness and breakouts on the skin are common in the early stages of a detoxing the body. Taking a sauna or sitting in a steam room will help open the pores, speed up the exit of toxins and allow the skin to clear faster. The result will be skin that's softer, clearer and smoother than when you started.

Detoxing gives you fresher breath

A backed up, sluggish colon can be a major contributor to bad breath, (halitosis). As the bowels begin to move more freely, which they do with the increase of soluble fibre from fruit and vegetables during a detox, the breath becomes cleaner.

Detoxing helps you kick bad habits

When we fast or detox, we eliminate many of the foods we eat simply out of habit and put healthier alternatives in their place. It's then often easier to stick to the newer, healthy habits than revert to the bad habits we've worked out of our systems. Drinking coffee and tea immediately after a detox, for example, will make you feel hyperactive, then fatigued. Drinking or eating dairy after eliminating it for a short period will leave thick mucus in your throat which you'll have got used not to feeling. And drinking more water will have hopefully trained your body to feel thirstier and demand more hydration than it got before.

Detoxing can help clear foggy heads and headaches

Many of the sugary, fat-laden foods we habitually eat during the day make us feel lethargic and foggy headed. The liver, having removed so many toxins from our body over time is overloaded, meaning that some toxins escape its processes and end up in the head area. This is a major reason for headaches and foggy heads. Once the liver can function more freely, all these stored toxins in the head will clear.

Detoxing promotes healthier hair and nail growth

Getting rid of toxins underneath the scalp at the point where hair follicles grow allows the follicle to receive more nutrients. Hair then grows faster and stronger and looks shinier and thicker. The same applies to the nails when liver function improves, as blood flowing to our extremities is now nutrient-rich.

Detoxing makes you feel lighter

With more fruit and vegetables in our diet during a detox, our colons are able to fully empty. This makes us feel lighter. There's also less likelihood of us overeating, which often makes us feel heavier and more sluggish.

Detoxing has anti-aging benefits

Toxins are a major factor in premature aging. They create free radicals, which can oxidise the cells in our body and age us. When we eliminate sugar, caffeine, alcohol, wheat, dairy and saturated fat from our diets, even if it's only periodically, the blood becomes less oxidised. This means we're less prone to free radical damage and have fresher, oxygenated, nutrient-rich blood reaching all our cells instead.

A suggested detox protocol

So, with the benefits of detoxing well established, let's take a look at a suggested detox protocol. As I recommended earlier, prepare for the detox by cutting coffee, alcohol, sugar, wheat, dairy, meat and tea from your diet for three days before you start. The same applies to packaged, boxed, canned or fast food.

Upon rising

Drink a large glass of warm boiled water with the juice of half a fresh lemon squeezed in.

Breakfast

Raw food should make up three quarters of your breakfast, so include things like:

- *Fruit (fresh or frozen)*
- *Raw organic rolled oats or oatmeal*
- *Plain organic live yoghurt*
- *Organic nuts and seeds*
- *Nut butters (cashew, almond and sesame)*
- *Nut milks such as almond, hazelnut and coconut*

Some of my favourite ways to use these ingredients are:

Fresh almond smoothie

Simply blend:
- *1 tablespoon of organic live yoghurt, cows, sheep, goats or soya**
- *1 cup of almond milk*
- *1 tsp of oatmeal*
- *1 tsp of ground almonds*

* live cultured dairy is preferable

Fresh berries with natural yoghurt

Take the fruit of your choice and cover with:
- *1 tablespoon of honey*
- *1 tablespoon of ground flaxseed*
- *3 tablespoons of organic whole porridge oats soaked for 15 minutes in almond milk to soften*
- *1 tablespoon of natural yoghurt*
- *1 tablespoon of toasted pumpkin seeds sprinkled over the top*

Organic oats with coconut and berries

All you need for this tasty dish is:
- *1 small cup of organic whole oats*
- *1 cup of water*
- *1 cup of almond or coconut milk*
- *1 teaspoon of tahini paste (sesame pulp)*

Warm the organic whole oats in the water and almond or coconut milk over a gentle heat. Add the tahini paste towards the end of cooking then serve over the berries. Add more coconut milk if you wish. Try to avoid using sweeteners other than maple syrup, brown rice syrup, brown malt syrup or agave syrup. Hopefully, though, the fresh fruit will be sweet enough.

To drink

Green or white tea and filtered water throughout the day.

Snacks

A snack between 10.00am and 11.00am will help to keep blood sugar levels stable and reduce the cravings that can occur during a detox. Any of these options will do the job:

- *A small handful of organic raw almonds*
- *Sliced apple or pear with some nut butter such as almond or hazelnut butter*
- *A banana*
- *A chopped carrot, some cucumber and celery with some good quality organic low fat hummus*
- *A freshly made juice such as carrot, apple, ginger, beetroot and celery*

Lunch

Aim for 60–80% raw food with added cooked grains, sweet potato or steamed fish to make up the balance. Try:

- *Raw vegetable salad with lettuce, cucumber, tomato, red onion, bell pepper and steamed broccoli with toasted pine, sesame or almond flakes on top. A dressing of one tablespoon of extra virgin olive oil, juice from a quarter of a lemon and sea salt can be added*
- *Sweet baked jacket potato with salad as above*
- *Steamed fish with brown basmati rice, quinoa or sweet potato with peas*
- *Lentils (puy) cooked in a tablespoon of Boullion powder and water for twenty minutes, added to lightly fried onions in virgin olive oil and garlic topped with seasonal steamed vegetables of your choice*
- *Steamed medley of vegetables served with either steamed fish or toasted nuts sprinkled on top to add flavour*

Afternoon snacks

Here are my three top detox afternoon snacks:

Mid pm smoothie, blend:

- *Almond milk*
- *Half a banana (or any fruit other than melon or grapes)*
- *1 tablespoon of mixed ground nuts*
- *1 tablespoon of natural low fat live yoghurt*
- *A dash of maple syrup to sweeten if necessary*

Nut and seed mix

Blend raw organic almonds with sunflower seeds, pumpkin seeds and chopped organic apricots, figs, dates or sultanas, for example. Avoid peanuts and macadamias as these are higher in saturated fat.

Two gluten-free crackers with a nut spread

As an alternative to gluten-free crackers, choose oatcakes. They contain gluten, but the good quality brands are fine.

Evening meal

These meal choices are ideal when you're detoxing:

- *Mixed vegetables with rice or quinoa*
- *1 cup of cooked brown rice or quinoa*
- *Chopped pepper*
- *Red onion with nuts over the top*
- *Carrot*
- *Sprouted beans (optional)*
- *Steamed broccoli*
- *Chopped tomato*

- *1 tablespoon of mixed chopped ground nuts or chia seeds*
- *Freshly squeezed lemon juice*
- *Teriyaki sauce*

Mix the rice or quinoa with the vegetables, then add the chopped ground nuts or chia seeds. Season with the freshly squeezed lemon juice and teriyaki sauce. Add sea salt if you wish.

Oven baked organic wild salmon

- *1 portion of wild organic salmon*
- *Fresh broccoli or bok choy*
- *1 small sweet potato*

Bake the sweet potato as you would a normal potato. Meanwhile wrap the salmon in foil and bake alongside the potato at 180º C for the last 25 minutes depending on its weight. Steam the broccoli or bok choy.

- *Mixed tinned bean salad*
- *1 tin of mixed bean salad*
- *Quinoa*
- *Raw chopped vegetables of your choice*
- *Sweet corn*
- *Toasted nuts of your choice*

Drain the beans well, mix well with the chopped vegetables, sweet corn and quinoa, then sprinkle toasted nuts of your choice.

A typical day on a juice fast	
8.00am	Green vegetable juice[1]
11.00am	Juice[2]
1.00pm	Juice[2]
3.00pm	Beetroot, carrot and apple juice
5.00pm	Juice[2]
6.00-8.00pm	Smoothie made with almond milk and berries

1. a juice made of carrots, celery, apple, pineapple, orange, beetroot, cucumber and leafy greens. Where possible, use organic fruit and vegetables. They won't have been treated with pesticides, so they won't have any chemical residue on their skin
2. kale, spinach, cucumber, green apple and celery

Pan roasted cashew nuts

- *1 cup of organic brown rice or quinoa*
- *Half a cup of pan roasted cashew nuts*
- *Bok choy*
- *Sweet potato cut into bite size chunks*
- *Broccoli*
- *Teriyaki sauce*

Cook the rice or quinoa and mix in the pan roasted cashew nuts. Steam the broccoli or bok choy and sweet potato. Serve with teriyaki sauce on top.

Follow this detox for between three to five days. If and when you reintroduce the foods you've eliminated back into your diet, do it gradually. Leave sugar, wheat, dairy, alcohol and coffee until the last possible day. Even then, don't add them all at once!

This is a good opportunity to consider whether you even want to go back to these foods and drinks. They are, after all the ones that built up the highest levels of toxins in the first place. As a compromise, you could decide to enjoy them again, but in lower quantities or less frequently.

If your lifestyle makes it impossible for you to follow the above detox, a juice fast may be the simpler option for you. You still eat your meals as normal, preferably with the toxic foods much reduced. You then take juices between meals.

If you can, think about replacing your last meal of the day with a juice. This will give the liver a good chance to fully cleanse and realign itself overnight without having to digest a heavy meal in the evening.

A more radical approach is to eliminate all solid foods and having juices in their place. Bear in mind, though, that raw organic juices contain nutrients, phytochemicals and anti-oxidants that we absorb easily when taken in liquid form. For this reason, it's unadvisable to do this type of fast for more than three days without the supervision of a qualified health care practitioner. It's also not recommended if you have a medical health condition. This kind of detoxification process can have affects that are extreme in some cases and, if a person's health is already compromised, it may not be able to cope with an extreme detox. If you do extend this fast beyond three days, include some light foods in your diet to curb your hunger.

There are specialist recipe books for different types of fasts, including juice fasting. It's a good idea to buy or borrow one of these, so you can follow your chosen fast correctly.

Preparing for a juice fast

It's essential to prepare for a juice fast for between one and four days before you start. Reduce your coffee, tea, sugar, wheat, dairy and alcohol intake gradually over these days to avoid severe withdrawal symptoms such as headaches, blood sugar level crashes, bloating and nausea. At the same time, you'll need to increase your water, fruit and vegetable consumption.

A typical day on a juice fast

Upon waking, have fresh lemon juice squeezed into some boiled water. This will expel any toxins that the liver is holding onto, enabling it to work more efficiently for the rest of the day. Then, for the most effective elimination of toxins, serve the juice at room temperature. For maximum absorption, drink it slowly.

You can prepare all your juices at the beginning of each day, or the evening before and store them overnight if that's easier. Bear in mind, though, that the nutrients start to break down immediately, so fresh is best. Ideally, store your juice in a glass or BPA-free bottle. BPA (Bis-phenol A) is an industrial chemical present in many hard plastic containers. It's been used since the 1960s, but in 2008, it was revealed that BPA can be harmful to human development and affect the brain and behaviour.

If you're aiming to go beyond a single day with your juice fast, you'll probably experience frequent - and possible uncomfortable – hunger. A simple, clear, homemade vegetable broth can help. If you're considering going for more than two days, it's a good idea to eat a fresh raw salad without dressing for lunch or your evening meal.

As with all forms of detox, reintroducing foods afterwards should be a slow and gradual process over three days to avoid a bad reaction.

Foods that detoxify

By regularly eating foods that naturally detoxify the body, we can prevent the build-up of toxins that make us feel sluggish and, eventually, unwell. Such foods include:

- *Onions and garlic – both of these contain sulphur, which helps facilitate the detoxification pathway for certain environmental chemicals, food additives and drugs*
- *Globe artichoke - this contains compounds called caffeoylquinic acids. These are believed to increase*

the flow of bile in our body and help break down unwanted fats
- *Beetroot – this also helps bile flow. It contains a compound called betaine, too. Betaine helps prevent fat from building up around our organs*
- *Broccoli – this supports liver detoxification enzymes. As the liver is the most important organ as far as detoxification goes, this is a good thing*

Common detoxifying foods by Sarah Burt

Supplements that support detoxing

You can supplement a detox or juice fast with:

- *Vitamin C – take 1000mg each morning to help reduce side effects such as headaches*

- *Inositol and choline - supplements that are lipotropic (ie they move fat) increase bile flow and help the detoxification process. Lecithin, a granular product found in health food shops, is an excellent source of both inositol and choline. Add 1 tablespoon of granules or a 1000mg capsule onto cereals daily to help gall bladder function*

STEP. 7
SUPERFOODS AND SUPERNUTRIENTS

From left to right: wheatgrass, chlorella and barley grass

As defined by the Macmillan Dictionary, a superfood is a food considered very good for your health and which may help with some medical conditions.

The Oxford English Dictionary defines a superfood as '... nutrient-rich food considered to be especially beneficial for health and wellbeing.'

Although there's no formal medical definition, super-foods contain concentrated levels of substances considered vital to good health. Examples include antioxidants, polyphenols, vitamins and minerals.

Superfoods are a special category of natural foods. By definition, they're calorie sparse and nutritionally dense. While we try to add more salads, fruit and vegetables to our diets, there's concern over the quality of the nutrients they provide. Our soil is overused, so its mineral density is compromised. As a result, the quality of the produce grown in this soil is not as good as it could be. So, by including superfoods in our diet, we can make up for this lack of essential vitamins and minerals and avoid unhealthy deficiencies.

There are five important superfood groups.

Green superfoods

Green superfoods have the highest concentrations of easily-digested nutrients, fat-burning compounds, vitamins and minerals to protect and heal the body.

They contain many beneficial substances, including proteins, protective phytochemicals and healthy bacteria. These help us build cleaner muscles and body tissue, aid the digestive system and protect against disease and illness. Examples of green superfoods include:

- *Wheatgrass - the sprouted grass of a wheat seed. Because it's sprouted, it doesn't contain gluten. Wheatgrass is strongly alkalising, so promotes healthy blood. It normalises the thyroid gland and stimulates metabolism*

- *Barley grass - this contains 11 times more calcium than cow's milk, five times more iron than spinach and seven times more vitamin C than orange juice. It contains significant levels of vitamin B12, so is great for vegetarians. Barley grass also neutralises heavy metals, such as mercury, in the bloodstream*

- *Spirulina - a cultivated micro-algae containing up to 70 per cent protein, making it one of the richest sources of protein on earth. With studies showing that spirulina helps control blood sugar levels and reduce sugar cravings, it's an excellent superfood for people with diabetes. Note: in some circumstances Spirulina may feed yeast and so best avoided by those with symptoms of candida*

- *Chlorella - a freshwater algae with a complete protein profile, this also contains B vitamins, vitamin C and vitamin E along with many minerals. Chlorella is proven to be good for reducing cholesterol levels, preventing arterial hardening and for the removal of heavy metals form the body*

From left to right: goji and acai berries, cocao powder and coconuts

Fruit and nut superfoods

Food and nut superfoods are very high in antioxidants that fight free radicals in our body. Free radicals form through natural occurrences such as metabolism, but too many of them can put a load on our bodies. We also acquire free radicals through pollution, smoking, eating burnt or deep fried food and having x-rays. When enough free radicals invade our immune system, problems start. Antioxidants fight off these free radical scavengers. Some great fruit and nut superfoods are:

- *Goji berries - grown on vines in valleys in Mongolia and Tibet, goji berries contain 500 times more vitamin C per ounce than oranges. They're also a good source of vitamins A, B1, B2, B6 and E. They contain 18 essential amino acids, so offer vegetarians a great source of protein. Goji berries contain over 21 trace minerals and are an excellent source of antioxidants*

- *Raw cocoa – this is possibly the world's most highly concentrated source of antioxidants. It's extremely high in magnesium, a mineral most western people are deficient in due to the reduced levels of it in our soil. Each serving of raw cocoa beans contains 21 per cent of the recommended daily allowance of iron and has 14 times more of the antioxidants known as flavonoids than red wine and 21 times more than green tea. Avoid cocoa beans that have been processed via the Dutch method. They'll have been subjected to temperatures of up to 150 degrees centigrade, which destroy most of the nutrients and antioxidants. Instead, buy a certified organic cocoa powder as the regulations governing its production limit processing temperatures to 40 degrees centigrade*

- *Maca powder - a powerful ancient superfood from Peru, consumed by the Inca warriors to increase their strength and endurance. This highly nutritious and widely available food supplement supports fertility and enhances immune function*

- *Acai berries – used as part of a ritual diet by tribes in the Amazon, acai berries contain powerful antioxidants, such as proanthocyanidins, which are also found in red wine. Try to buy them freeze-dried as this preserves most of their nutrients*

- *Coconuts - young coconuts are one of nature's richest source of electrolytes. These transport high quality energy around our body and are much better than commercial sports drinks at replacing electrolytes lost through exercise and perspiration. The molecular structure of coconut water is identical to that of human blood plasma, so drinking it is like giving your body an instant transfusion! In fact, it was used to give emergency blood transfusions to wounded soldiers in the Second World War*

- *Coconut oil – the fat in coconuts is a medium-chain-fatty acid. This means it's digested more easily and is used differently by the body than saturated fats, such as butter, cheese and cream. Fat from coconut oil is sent straight to the liver, where it's immediately converted into energy rather than being stored. It can speed up metabolism, allowing the body to burn more calories throughout the day. Containing anti-bacterial, antifungal and antiviral agents, coconut oil is hailed as a cure all gift from nature by the Pacific Islanders*

Worker bee saturated with pollen

Bee superfoods

- *Royal jelly - a milk-like secretion from the head gland of the worker bees. The queen bee, who lives around*

40 times longer than all the other bees, lives almost entirely on this. Royal jelly is the world's richest source of vitamin B5, which helps to combat stress, fatigued adrenals, tiredness and insomnia, so is the ideal supplement for our busy, modern lifestyles

- *Bee pollen – nature's most complete food, this has between five and seven times more protein than beef. It's especially beneficial for athletes and any anyone recovering from illness. It's a natural antidote for allergies such as hay fever and good generally for the sinuses*

- *Propolis – used by bees to coat the walls of their hives - making them among the most antiseptic environments in nature – this works against viruses and reduces the frequency of coughs and colds if taken in winter*

Bee propolis

Seaweed superfoods

Absorbing all the nutrients the oceans provide, seaweed is one of the most nutritionally dense plants on the planet and one of the most abundant sources of minerals in the plant kingdom.

Seaweed contains up to ten times more calcium than milk. It's very close in concentration to blood plasma so is excellent at regulating and purifying our blood. And, being highly alkalising, it helps neutralise excess acid in the body.

Seaweed also has chelating properties. This means it converts harmful environmental toxins, heavy metals and other pollutants in the body into harmless salts that we can excrete.

Seaweed is very rich in chlorophyll, which helps to detoxify the body, while its high levels of iodine help stimulate the thyroid gland and maintain healthy metabolism. Seaweed can also help prevent cholesterol building up in our bodies.

Excellent sources of seaweed are:

- *Nori - best known as an ingredient of sushi rolls. Use the untoasted sheet for maximum nutritional benefit*

- *Kelp - also available in supplement form, this thicker seaweed is often used for hot seaweed baths*

- *Dulse - a red seaweed that you can buy in flakes and add straight into any meal and sprinkle over salads, vegetables and soups*

- *Arame - this black stringy seaweed needs to be soaked for five minutes before adding to cooking. It's used widely in stir fries*

- *Wakame - sold fresh or dehydrated and best sprinkled in soups, stocks, stews or stir fries*

- *Kombu - a mineral-rich flavour enhancer which, when added to beans during cooking, makes them easier to digest*

From left to right: arame, kelp, wakame and dulse seaweed

When buying seaweeds, look for organic brands. The quality of the product depends on the quality of the water it grew in.

Herbal superfoods

Herbs contain nutrients that have been used for centuries for their natural healing abilities and body balancing properties. They're best taken in their whole form, ie without any of their constituents extracted or concentrated. My four top herbal superfoods are:

- *Urtica dioica (nettle) - incredibly effective in removing unwanted pounds, as a cup of fresh or dried nettle tea in the morning helps to promote regular bowel habits. Nettle is also known to increase metabolism as it stimulates the thyroid gland*

- *Aloe vera – this contains over 75 natural healing compounds, including natural steroids, antibiotic agents, amino acids, minerals and enzymes. It's high in sulphur, which is great for all skin conditions. Aloe also alkalises the digestive tract, preventing indigestion, reflux, heartburn and ulcers and helping IBS*

From left to right: aloe, ginseng, holy basil and nettle

- *Echinacea angustifolia - this is known as an immune stimulant due to its ability to promote lymph flow and carry toxins out of the body. It can be taken in liquid, tablet or capsule form for a few weeks at a time during flu season or in tea form, which you can drink daily*

- *Panax ginseng - available in many different varieties, all known to reduce – and help our bodies cope with – stress. Varieties include: Siberian / Korean ginseng*

- *Astragalus membranaceous - Most commonly used for strengthening the immune system. This does, over time building our body's resistance to illness and disease. It also shows to improve function of the cardiovascular system, especially where there is myocardial infarct (destruction of the structure of the heart). In Chinese herbal medicine its used to treat Hepatitis. It is also useful in the treatment of the common cold, and is considered to be completely safe and free of side effects*

- *Withania somnifera - ashwaganda, or Indian ginseng, poison gooseberry, winter cherry. Part of the solanceae or deadly nightshade family. It has been used for over 3000 years in the oldest medicine* system in the world, Āyurveda. Its main effect is to restore vitality and vigour to those lacking in energy as it stimulates the immune system and nourishes the adrenal glands

- *Rhodiola rosea (golden rose) - another great tonic to restore strength and balance and was originally used by the Vikings to give them strength and courage. More recently used by the Russians in the Cold War. It grows only in extreme climates*

- *Glycyrrhiza glabra (liquorice) - known to be useful in so many ways. It seems to prevent the breakdown of adrenal hormones making them more available in the body. It is also a well documented stomach ulcer healer, as it lowers stomach acid, and is hailed too for its potential to fight tooth decay. It has an aspirin like action and helps relieves fevers and soothes such pains as headache pains. It is useful for hayfever, allergies and asthma. It helps with these conditions due to its nickname as natures steroid, and acts to bring down excess inflammation in all these conditions. It boosts levels of interferon which is a key immune chemical which attacks viruses. It can dislodge excess mucus in our respiratory tracts thus making it very soothing in hacking dry coughs. Studies have also shown that it protects the liver and prevents heart disease by limiting the damage that bad fats do on the arteries*

- *Schisandra chinensis - the ultimate super berry, not eaten but used instead for medicinal purposes alone.*

It is a sweet, sour, salty, bitter and pungent tasting berry, and therefore is known in Chinese medicine as the five flavoured berry. It is native to North China and used much in Traditional Chinese medicine as a immune stimulant and anti-inflammatory. It improves energy and mental health

- *Lycium Barbarum (wolf berry), one of the most powerful plants used in herbal medicine, traditionally used in Tibetan medicine and Traditional Chinese medicine , and in Tibet was named the 'key to eternal youth'. It has one of the highest vitamin C contents of any fruit in the world, therefore is a powerful anti oxidant. It is also known for its ability to restore the immune system*

- *Ocimum sanctum (holy basil) is a member of the mint family. Also known as Tulsi has been used for fertility treatment in Ãyurvedic medicine. Being an adaptogenic herbs it also reduces the effects of stress on the body*

Ganoderma lucidum (reshi mushroom) by Sarah Burt

- *Ganoderma lucidum (reishi mushroom), is said to have miraculous health benefits. It can be taken daily and when taken regularly can restore the body to its natural state, enabling all organs to function normally. Made up mainly of complex carbohydrates called polysaccharides which are known to be the most helpful in anti-tumour and immune stimulating properties. The evidence of these properties comes from studies done in Japan, China and the USA*

THE END

Osteoporosis (page 27)
A disorder in which the bones become increasingly porous, brittle, and subject to fracture owing to loss of calcium.

Bursitis (page 31)
Inflammation of the Bursa which is a pouch containing fluid which allows movement between a bone and tendon.

Microbes
A pathogenic microorganism.

Adenoids (page 32)
An enlarged mass of lymphatic tissue in the upper throat area.

Appendix
Part of the endocrine system, a gland positioned above the pubic area.

Emulsifier (page 34)
A substance which has the ability to change the chemical disposition of (in this case) fat to make it more easily absorbed.

Viscosity (apge 41)
The word used to describe the thickness of a fluid by the rate at which it flows.

GLOSSARY

Cortisol (page 45)
One of the several steroid hormones produced by the adrenal cortex.

Philosophy (page 51)
A particular system of thought based on study or investigation.

Diaphragmatic breaths (page 53)
Also known as 'belly breathing', is breathing done by contracting the muscle located between the thoracic cavity and abdominal cavity, thus expanding the abdomen rather than the chest when practiced.

Hair follicles (page 72)
A skin organ that produces hair.

Quinoa (page 76)
A grain crop similar to buckwheat, known as a pseudocereal, grown for its edible seeds. Cooked in the same way as rice, nutritionally high in protein.

Puy lentils
A particular strain of lentils grown in Portugal Le Puy.

Bok choy (page 79)
A type of Chinese cabbage, also known as pak choy or chinese chard.

Phytochemicals (page 80)
Chemical compounds that occur naturally in plants, some are responsible for the deep colour in fruits and vegetables, (e.g the purple in blueberries) or the smell such as that of garlic.

Polyphenols (page 85)
The term should be used to define compounds which feature more than one phenolic unit that are naturally found and not man made.

Electrolytes (page 88)
Is a substance that produces and electrically conducting solution when dissolved in a polar solvent such as water.

BIBLIOGRAPHY

Alkalize or die
Dr Theodore A Baroody

The pH Miracle
Robert O. Young and Shelley Redford Young

The Liver Cleansing Diet
Dr Sandra Cabot

It's so natural
Alan Hayes

Food is better medicine than drugs
Patrick Holford and Jerome Burne

The Encyclopaedia of Healing Foods
Dr Michael Murray and Joseph Pizzorno

The Complete Guide to Modern Herbalism
Simon Mills

The True Power of Water
Masaru Emoto

NOTES

NOTES

Made in the USA
Charleston, SC
27 December 2016